G000124253

Killdeer

Phil Hall · Killdeer

ESSAY-POEMS

BookThug

Cover image (detail) by John James Audubon [Engraver: Robert Havell]: CCXXV
(225). Plate Caption: Kildeer Plover, Charadrius vociferus. 1, Male. 2, Female. 1834

www.bookthug.ca

The production of this book was made possible through the generous assistance
of the Ontario Arts Council and the Canada Council for the Arts.

 ONTARIO ARTS COUNCIL
CONSEIL DES ARTS DE L'ONTARIO

 Canada Council   Conseil des Arts
for the Arts   du Canada

LIBRARY AND ARCHIVES CANADA CATALOGUING IN PUBLICATION

Hall, Phil, 1953–
  Killdeer/ Phil Hall.

(Department of critical thought; no. 4)
  Poems.
ISBN 978-1-897388-81-5

I. Title. II. Series: Department of critical thought; no. 4

PS8565.A449K55 2011   C811'.54   C2011-901290-1

PRINTED IN CANADA

Don't repent. Don't manage. Essay.

HÉLÈNE CIXOUS

Contents

Killdeer

Adios Polka

Whenever I get lost
Ontario does not wound me

the mewl & skitter of the half-eyes at the registries

have defined distance as health – & nostalgia
as a gossamer sac writhing with tent-worms

(flutter-smeared & eaten green the wild grapes)

these slips booklet-stipends collectible-spills curios
I balance a fortress of / if I must be home / *be hame*

are apolitical except in their endurance

it has rained 3 days & these pioneer logs are sponges
maps out-of-date unhinged on the pine floor

(wide first-growth planed buttery / *laned uttery*)

there is nowhere to go off
but wordward

Bess & Lloyd

When my wife's Aunt Bess moved herself into Bridlewood (&
hung the huge Karsh print of her dead husband – Ross – on the
wall beside her bed)

She re-met another good man there from her school days – Lloyd
– a widower dapper going blind – they had danced once long ago

Although he had been assigned to a different table in the dining
room – at each meal he held her chair out for her – then went
back to his own

And boy did the tongues around that place ever wag

They both hated it there – it was costing them a fortune – two
fortunes – so they moved out & bought a high-rise condo
downtown Brockville overlooking the St Lawrence

They could see the tankers going up & down river – & across the
way – *Amurrica*

They even renovated – had a service window installed between the
little kitchen & the dining table – to save steps

*

Now they are on their balcony – staring down at their shaky blue
pool – it comes with the condo & is right beside the dark Seaway

The river's whitecaps hiss in a foreign wind that yanks the hair on
their heads back mercilessly

A deer is in the pool – has jumped the wooden fence & torn its
hind-leg – blood swirling around it as it swims

Leaning out from the railing they take turns using Lloyd's big
binoculars – each time they pass the glasses between them they
are careful to put the strap again over their heads

The circles merge to show the deer's tail – a flag – up-close soggy
faintly blue heavy – a swab lolling in chlorine

*

Later – Bess phones us – when we call back – Lloyd answers – *Joe's Pool Hall*

How in God's name did it ever get down to the water through all that city – why jump that fence – did no one notice it till now – wasn't it scared – or scared enough

Oh – yeah – really – Bess says – excitedly confused – then nervously bursts out laughing like a schoolteacher at a skating party – then puts a hand to her throat to interrupt the laugh – coy

*

You know Bess has moved back into Bridlewood – how her husband Ross's Karsh photo is back up beside her bed – how daily she takes the Wheel-Trans to visit Lloyd who is pretty-well bed-ridden – he's in a nursing home not too far away

What you don't know is that for now Bess is keeping the condo as is – for her daughter Judith – who lives in Fort McMurray – to stay in when she visits – & that the empty rooms – looking out over the choppy Seaway – are hung with stunning Canadian paintings & prints by William Kurelek – David Blackwood – Mary Pratt – Allen Sapp

What you don't know is that Bess has a younger brother – Howard – who is getting up there too – this summer he is selling his farm & having an auction sale that we won't miss – then he is moving into Bridlewood also – he is going to share a double suite with his sister

Howard's a great pie-maker – & where he's going to make pies now is the question we are all asking ourselves

~

Becoming A Poet

A

On a Sunday morning in July 1973 I hitchhiked from Bobcaygeon
to Lakefield to meet Margaret Laurence

When a ride let me off in Buckhorn I had breakfast at a counter
on stools among fishermen – my eggs were scrambled & served by
a one-armed man

I got to Lakefield about 10:00 – most people up that early were in
church – I had a clipping from *The Globe and Mail* – a photograph
of Laurence's house

The Diviners had just been published – I had a copy with me – the
first new hardback I ever bought

With the photo to help me I meant to find Laurence's house &
just knock

The previous winter I had finished my first year at the University
of Windsor – where my English professor – Dr Huong – had said
– without any hint of a question – *You don't know how to write a
sentence do you*

Nevertheless – even as I walked around Lakefield – my first little
book of adolescent poems was being typeset atrociously in
Mexico City

I can't remember now what possessed me to seek out Laurence –
but I hope it possesses me still

It wasn't that I particularly cherished her writing – then – I was
too inflated & dazed – having *left the farm* – having *gone away to
university*

As maudlin as it sounds – of many generations of drunks I was the
first to ever finish high school

Because of the imminent First Book I thought of Laurence & I as
colleagues

Besides – she was living nearby in Lakefield now – & this
proximity suggested family to me at nineteen

I had already begun to hunt for & invent a literary family to
replace the one I had been born into & couldn't abide

*

She wasn't home – I knocked – twice – but not too hard – I was
eager to hurry away – maybe it was the wrong house – was it too
early – had she gone to church

I walked around the cemetery for an hour reading the stones
(there were no Halls) & when I knocked again at 11:00 the door
opened

An Eskimo woman in a patterned shift stood there smoking a flat cigarette – when she spoke I saw that her teeth were black

Her words were delivered with a confident slur & there was no poise – I loved her instantly

My dead mother's teeth & smokes were the same

I apologized for knocking – for the early hour – for knocking earlier – for being there at all

Laurence seemed eager that I come in – she said she would like me to phone next time

Next time – was I to be a regular visitor – then – so easily

No – she was not addressing me specifically – but giving general advice to the numbers of visitors she had started getting lately – now that she was famous – even notorious – because of *The Diviners*

*

I've just finished wallpapering under the stairs here – & this wall – do you like it

Was the wall cream-coloured with purple irises – what did I know about home decorating

My mother used to buy plastic curtains

My dad & his girlfriend were having straight vodka for brunch
right now in the ramshackle Iroquois Apartments in Bobcaygeon

I bought this the other day – too – & I think it goes so well against the
new wallpaper here below the stairs – I'm not sure what you call these

It's a chair – & the seat lifts up – so there's storage underneath – & the
back of the chair has this bevelled mirror – & there's these coat hooks up
here on both sides

There must be an actual name – it's lovely – do you think – oak

Yes – to me furniture was still bricks & milk crates

What I *could* understand was this woman's simple loneliness on a
Sunday morning – her eagerness to find approval – & her pride in
her home

I was ashamed to recognize what I thought of as weaknesses in her
– I had no right – & they were not weaknesses

Now I know that if she could entrust her vulnerabilities to even
me she must have taken the same risks with everyone – from her
children outward to glomming strangers

She risked a generous grace

*

I want to go back & protect her from the likes of me

Her cat's name was Amber – her rowboat – that her son had
painted for her – was named *C C Grant* – this she told as a
rehearsed joke

*My son is worried that if the boat ever gets away in a flood I'll never get it
back because they'll think its owner's name is C C Grant when really the C
C stands for Canada Council – Canada Council Grant – which is what
paid for it*

She ended with a slight drawl & swagger – held the moment –
then punctuated it with a final drag on her cigarette – a side drag

I didn't laugh when I should have because I didn't know what a
Canada Council Grant was

To cover for myself – I reaching into my yellow Army Surplus
shoulder bag – pulled out my copy of *The Diviners* & asked if she
would sign it for me

I also handed her poems – far too many – a crumpled bundle – I
knew she didn't write poems – I didn't care

She said that she didn't write poems but that she would read them
& write me a letter about them

I thanked her & left – the hitchhike home took longer – the day
was hotter – memory fails – having caught its limit

*

Eventually I got a typed letter from Laurence – she was too kind – I have so often put that letter in a special place for safekeeping that I forget where it is

It is somewhere – one of the reasons I write is because it is somewhere

When I want to revisit that meeting I rent & watch the N F B film *First Lady of Manawaka* or the shorter version for schools called *Our Kinda Talk*

The home interviews for that documentary must have been done shortly after *The Diviners* was published – so about the same time as my pilgrimage to Laurence's house

The way she says *darn sure* chokes me up

*

It is by such encounters – brash – rude – naive – foolhardy or accidental – that we discover or select our lineages as writers

(I think – too – of Dorothy Livesay – late in life – stooping to touch my daughter's hand – blessing her)

Margaret Laurence touched the hand I write with – otherwise my pen might belong nowhere – have no family – be part of no continuance

She touched many – deeply – & me merely in passing – but
without her touch I might be as if one-armed

I would have to hit myself to clap

I might be silent

B

My first year at university – I met a graduate student named
David Marley whose father was the Director of Cyanamid Mining
Company in Mexico

Marley had been translating old Spanish mining texts into English
& using Cyanamid's advertising budget to produce elegant
booklets decorated with Aztec symbols – his father had been
giving these to delegates at mining conventions

With his black-framed glasses – kinky red hair – & sunless skin
– Marley looked like Michael Caine in *Funeral In Berlin* – he was
Canadian – but had been raised in Mexico City

This all seemed very exotic to me – David was my Oxford – he
lived in a two-room-with-bath graduate flat in one of the old
Basilian Fathers buildings

In the entrance lobby there were dreadful portraits of academic
priests – even I could see that they were flat & unrelentingly
brown

Wyndham Lewis had painted them when he taught there in the
early 1940s

On Sundays David took me to play chess with silent pipe-smoking
Egyptians

As his sidekick I slept through Kenneth Clark's *Civilisation* series when it was screened by reel-to-reel projector successive Friday afternoons in the fledgling Women's Studies Office

Marley had me categorized as an indigenous primitive – a colonial John Clare – I encouraged this interpretation – he wanted to try *something literary* with his father's company's money – so a book of poems of mine became his project

I stole the title – *Eighteen Poems* – from Dylan Thomas's first book

*

One of the poems in *Eighteen Poems* is about Irving Layton – whose *Lovers and Lesser Men* had come out that year

On the cover – there's Layton as minotaur – hairy-chested – sporting a medallion

Every young poet then had a poem about Irving Layton – mine went – *you would pee/in God's eye/if he tried to change you*

This pathetic Layton poem was also one of the ones I had thrust shakily into the hands of Margaret Laurence

Well – that summer – while I was washing dishes in the El Toro Steak House back home – Marley sent my Irving Layton poem to Irving Layton

Eventually – from Greece – I got a postcard from Layton

Yes – he said – he *would* pee in God's eye if God tried to change him

He liked the poem – & why didn't I send it to *Waves* – the literary magazine at York University

Hey – in the letter I had gotten from Margaret Laurence there was the same suggestion – why didn't I send my Layton poem to *Waves*

So I did – no gods to grab my hair – my first submission to a literary journal

C

My poems were sent back with a rejection slip from *Waves* – even my cover letter was returned

In my ignorance – what I had said in my cover letter was – *Both Irving Layton & Margaret Laurence have recommended I send these poems to you* – (OK a slight lie)

In the margin – in faint pencil – one of the editors had quipped – *Well I want Trudeau to like them too*

Nothing has ever so stabbed home to me the folly of ambition

By failing to erase that joke between editors – someone rescued me from years of ass-kissing

I longed to be a writer before I felt driven to write

I got a degree in writing – & I published a first book – way before writing became my compulsive practice

Since then I have learned to always put the art before the course

*

Eighteen Poems arrived in a box on a bus from Mexico City

The cover is a grey watercolour of a foggy shore – *Holiday Beach* – by E. A. Hodgkinson – Marley's uncle

Inside – old Mexican woodcuts designate sections – (but of course the book is too small for sections)

I spread the copies out on my cot in residence – like an animal come down to water to drink from its own image – I got on my knees & smelled those books

The printer's ink – the oil of the cutting machine – the dusty underbelly of the United States by Greyhound – these were the ingredients I smelled

But my snout also caught a glorious whiff of the death of my past

I thought I had killed off all that haunted me by writing well

I had written atrociously – & my doodling toward islands of repair – hadn't even begun yet

*

Indefatigably – Marley sent 100 copies of *Eighteen Poems* to writers across Canada

The only letter I got in response came from George Amabile at the University of Manitoba

He said – *Far from giving me any pleasure this book almost made me puke – if I were you I wouldn't write another book for 10 years*

I was 20 – that letter broke my stupid heart

I swore that if I ever met George Amabile I would punch him in the nose

A few years later I did meet him – at *The Great Canadian Poetry Weekend* near Collingwood – Ontario – one summer – maybe 1975

Those really were great weekends – poets would fly in from all over Canada – & a bus would bring them from Toronto airport north to the Blue Mountain ski hills

I would hitchhike there & sleep in a tent just to be near the stars

Al Purdy was playing pool – trumpeting his deep deflective *Ahhh* – sweeping his hair back off that high forehead – his shirt-tails out

Atwood – in a green cape – with an entourage – swept through at 10:30 sharp – paused to laugh once – with *Duende* – & then was gone

Acorn was frothing – upset about another travesty of politics by art – or of art by politics – or both – no one could afford to appear to be listening to him – (then or now)

Jay Macpherson's astute silence anchored a room – a classical / demure dingbat – she crouched & listened – in a head-scarf

Dennis Lee got pounding out hard honky-tonk piano – rocking from side-to-side – baring his bad teeth – calling down Fats Waller from the wooden rafters

A moth landed on Joe Rosenblatt while he was humming like a bee – but the audience wasn't watching – because out the window – over his shoulder – we could all see bare arms & legs in an amorous clench in the tall grass up the mountainside

George Amabile didn't remember the book or my name or the letter he had sent

He was playing guitar & singing with others in a circle on the hillside – he offered me a beer – I liked him

I sat down & sang – I joined my tribe – the punch went inward

D

As it turned out – I *wouldn't* publish another book for 10 years

I pulled my neck way in & began to write – not for Layton – Laurence – or Amabile

Not for the gods & goddesses of any English Department

Not for approval – but for survival – though I don't want to leave the impression that I was being noble in retreat

That I had gone off bruised into my little wilderness to plot a triumphant return

I muddled through – continued to send poems to magazines – & sometimes one got accepted

Writing was seldom the main thing that was going on – I was too off-balance & scared to have a regular rhythm to my days

I worked on outlandish – presumptuous – silly – imitative long poems

I revised them to death – they croaked from eating scribble

*

Gradually – my first actual poems began to show themselves – as cringing & bounding fragments

When I close my eyes – I can see them – as they first came to me

Trepidation swoops low over a specific lot on the 9th Concession

I can hear old fiddle tunes – pluck & moan – & animal noises – bounce & skate

Not language yet – but wafted nodules of rhythm – caught in cross-hatch

Not form – or content – so much as toned designations of space

Overlapping risks of grey & green

*

By focus – to tip sensed textures – toward invitation & conduit

~

Twenty Lost Years

Two brothers start school – the teacher asks their names – *Lester B Pearson-Smith – John Diefenbaker-Smith*

Really – well – that couldn't be their names – but they insist – so the teacher calls the mother

That's right – says the mother – *when I had the boys – I wasn't married – & I couldn't think of a better pair of names for a couple of bastards*

*

Voice is a solid – a volatile solid

Our speech – like stone & clay – is a *time-biased* medium – Harold Innis says

It endures over time – & is traditionally associated with what is customary – sacred – moral

Speech is a time-biased solid because it requires & nurtures the stability of a community by actual human interchange

Face-to-face know-how – passed down orally – from one person you'd trust with your life – to another you wouldn't trust as far as

There is no dialogue between sentences – Bakhtin interjects

Utterance not sentence

*

*For Innis – the organization of empires seems to follow two major models –
the first model is militaristic & concerned with the conquest of space – the
second model is religious & concerned with the conquest of time*
(DAVID GODFREY)

*

Innis argues that while the oral tradition is time-biased – flexible
– yet a solid

The written tradition – from papyrus to pop-up – is rigid &
impersonal – *space-biased*

He warns us about an advertising-driven media obsessed by
present-mindedness – *& the continuous – systematic – ruthless
destruction of elements of permanence essential to cultural activity*

*

Marshall McLuhan refers to Innis's *mosaic* writing style

The interaction of substances in a mutual irritation

*In writing – the tendency is to isolate an aspect of some matter
& to direct steady attention upon that aspect*

In dialogue – in contrast – there tends to be an *interplay of
multiple aspects*

34

*

Tongue on paper – voice – not invoice

Bronwen Wallace knew instinctively what Innis & McLuhan
explain

She understood the good balance to be struck between talking &
writing – (the letter)

Between speech & text – (the lyric) – between oral history & the
document – (Livesay's *Documentaries*)

Sigmund Freud died of cancer of the mouth – as did Ivan Illich –
& Bron

Psychoanalysis – Liberation Theology – *our kinda talk*

The tongue is a stele – lash & groove

*

Bron Wallace came knocking – up our back stairs – the night my
son was born

Raspberry leaf tea – for the contractions – she said to my wife – Cathy

Look at this poem – she said to me – a typewritten page

It was the one we all know now – the one she ends by dipping her cigarette in her coffee & starting to write

*

Gary Snyder says – it doesn't matter where you draw the line – your line – the important thing is that you draw one – that you won't cross – like in Westerns

He says – when you do that – your little mark in the sand instantly links up with all of the other lines that are being drawn – they amount to one line

A unified front against bad food – bad government – bad water – bad writing – (the cheating arts)

But I didn't learn this from Snyder – I learned this from Bron – she scraped (& wrote) many lines that she stood behind – many at once

*

When I met her – I was still scrambling to maintain physical & mental autonomy – balance enough to call myself a poet

Bron was doing shifts at a collective political bookstore – & at a parent-run day care that she had helped found – she was enthusiastic about Lamaze birthing methods – having recently laboured a child that way – Jeremy

She was arguing regional politics along with national integrity
over beer

Her partner – Ron Baxter – worked for the Post Office – nights –
he had organized a discussion group – they met on break – their
texts were the journals they sorted & borrowed – read – discussed
– & then sorted back into the system

We lived in the same house for a while – in Windsor – upstairs
& downstairs apartments – we were in the same graduate poetry
workshop run by Eugene McNamara at the University of Windsor

*

Maybe I was her first poetry editor – because that year
(1977) I edited the student literary journal – *Generation* – an
embarrassment – except for Bron's poems

She had been drawing so many lines for so long that when she
came to *writing* some they came out full-blown – ripe – sure

She doesn't seem to have known she was a writer until she *was* a
writer – a good one – with almost no embarrassing juvenilia to
stumble through

*

I have built a way forward with poems using doubt

But I have Bron's absolute confidence in all of us with me each
day as I tinker

She believed in a unified front against despair – because she did –
I do – mostly

Sometimes – even now – 20 years later – when I've finished a
poem – or think I have – I think – *Bron would like this*

Or – *I'd have a fun old time arguing with Bron about this one*

*

She was no saint – she could be blunt or crude or goofy – hers was
an awkward beauty – absent of diversion

Unbudgeable communal faith together with usual-headedness –
she had all that – as her poems do

I write poems so that if she were to knock again – I'll have some

*

The 1957 election was the Canadian people's last gasp of nationalism

George Grant – in *Lament for a Nation* – tells how Diefenbaker &
his Conservative government – between 1957 & 1965 – made the
last charge in defence of Canada as an autonomous nation

But by then – Grant says – it was a done deal – *for twenty years before
its defeat in 1957 – the Liberal party had been pursuing policies that led
inexorably to the disappearance of Canada*

I would frame Canadian nationalism's decreasingly hopeful
heyday between Diefenbaker's first huge majority election win
that year & a final symbolic knell in 1994 at the signing of the
NAFTA agreement

Mulroney & Reagan singing together at the White House

(The windfall of Canadian literature in the '60s & '70s – was a
crop from an already toppled tree)

*

Bron was born in 1945 – she was 12 in 1957 when Diefenbaker
came to power – she was 20 in 1965 – she began publishing in the
'70s – she died in 1989

She coincides with Canadian literary nationalism – was a believer
– the last fresh carrier of our optimism – an activist

But not an idealist – she was too *time-biased* for that

*

Everyone at once who was standing on poems then heard
Wallace's voice – we were invigorated by its widening patterns

She carried her regionalism so effortlessly – made it sound
encompassing – place & voice – wherewithal & come-to-roost

Just maybe hers was a voice that could represent us – especially
women – carry forward the tattered standard

Unite us in its humanism – like Purdy's but a woman's – like
Livesay's but funkier

*

Then the voice rotted out from under us & was gone

No one since has tried to speak as familiarly to us – in poems

No one will – no one wants to anymore – it's every poem for itself

The New Internationalism has no time to sit down & yack

*

When a Wallace poem says *I* – it means *me Bronwen*

That's not cool anymore – but that's what she was leading with –
herself – herself *among*

Of course her *I* also means *this woman you know who is like yourself*

Her *I* is both herself & a character much like herself – like you & me – men too

A mask – but not a stage mask – not designed or styled – more of a no-make-up-on-yet composite

A hopeful & complex human sort we would all like to see a bit of ourselves in

The woman who is the poem is a mixture of intrigued & baffled – alone & surging with company – an anecdote-hound

Get in here for god's sake & tell me all about it right now

*

We know Bron when we hear her – but we also know now that the first person pronoun is a floater – it hovers – nowhere – it is not the poet

No – it is not the poet – soon after Al Purdy dies he stops sounding like *the voice of the land*

He isn't around to sustain his poems with the legend of his personality

(A trademark swagger of indifference – that bluff & huff – drops away – we fall from shrug to *gravitas* – & the poems – almost embarrassingly – open their profundity)

No – it is not the poet – Wallace's poems too have begun to ring hollow

If she came to class & read to students her poem *Gifts* – the one where her son is crying upstairs during her birthday party because he has bought her a t-shirt that is not *her* & too small

Sure they'd get its complexity of emotions – they would hear how it is about

But there's been a shift – & this is not only pronouns – this is the dilution of political *savvy* – a redefining of *citizens* as *consumers*

Where students used to be eager to discuss their own kids or memories – the whole nature of gifts

They now get into a discussion about – *why doesn't she just return the stupid shirt*

Which will lead to marketing & easy on-line return policies – (I'm not kidding)

*

The comfort of a friend in a poem – is an illusion

No solution or agreeable shrug – no roundedness or summing up

The Cold of Poetry – as Lyn Hejinian puts it

Yes – closure can be an immense larynx-trap – a reactionary *cul de sac* – as Bron knew too

But we miss our friend – even as we float our pronouns – even as we seek non-closure

The inclusive comfort of what's shared (besides language) has been foregone

We miss a voice like Wallace's – she was good at intense associations followed by you-&-me-both-pal smiles

*

We all know that if Bron had lived she would have become a novelist

For her – as with so many of our best poets – the poem fast became too constraining

Her last poems seem to have endings imposed on them – they want to keep going – talking all night

Therefore – the prose poems – the columns – the short stories

Who inherits her voice – who keeps its perspicuity going

I read to find the traces of her – & each time I hear her tone in poems she didn't write – I like to think we aren't completely hopeless

That our story-pulse may be volatile yet

*

In 1951 – Margaret Avison wrote a public school textbook – a
history of Ontario

(Avison born 1918 – Edith Fowke 1913 – Dorothy Livesay 1909 –
Helen Creighton 1899)

In 1951 – letters were a sort of money – they were saved – re-read
– inherited

Diaries mushroomed with ink splotches – Bron was six – her
grandmothers were busy – gathering & listening – curious &
inclusive

*

We learned to read from *Readers* that were Grey Owl-ish – British
in tone but including Canadian themes

We were given covers for our *Readers* – paper placemats we folded
as instructed – the front & back panels of a book slid into sleeves

Here's one of those jackets – blotter-paperish – blue – a map
of Northern Canada – the Yukon & the Northwest Territories –
regional crests

Plus a third crest – a *Coca-Cola* symbol – *Northern Canada – Our
Rich Frontier – you may be one of the pioneers of the new North* – a bottle
of Coke

A *Roads to Resources* program – the DEW Line – a cover – for a
book – sure – but its enthusiasm about the North is a cover for
economic take-over too

A promotional gift – propaganda for a done deal – the line blank
where a student might write her name – as if joining some corps

*

For Bron – it's not just – *once upon a time*

She can't tell the story without telling how it is being told

I hear my friend Rhonda reading her daughter Alice to sleep

Once upon a time there was a fish who granted a man three wishes

As I am trying to remember what the wishes are – I hear the train go by

And think of John Fogerty – Big Train From Memphis – he means Elvis

*Once Alice is asleep – her mom & I will talk about our troubles – again –
late into the night*

*The night – which is a whole other story altogether – or the same one but
looser*

The jumble we just can't throw out

*

Why not – well – if it weren't for this narrative jumble – told &
retold – despair would flare through – unmuffled

Almost everyone in Bron's poems has cancer – something hunts
us down & wins even as we defy the odds

Cancer is a train you may not be on today – but you will probably
get on board – eventually

So put on Emmy Lou Harris – or Elvis again – get on that big
train – *& ride*

Even the way folks talk about their cancers – is *kinda* optimistic –
in a resigned way

Like – *I have to go to Montreal for the weekend – can you feed my fish
while I'm away* – like that – & we will – we did – we are

Though the magic is dead inside the wishes – & the tracks empty

*

As you can see – one of Bron's talents was for weaving disparate types
into community – *the interaction of substances in a mutual irritation*

Twenty years later – we who knew her – we who only know her by
loving her poems – are in this far-flung ditch together – a vinyl
(blue flickering) groove

46

Though the possessive plural – *our* – is increasingly debatable –
even from ethnic or class perspectives

*Where can people learn independent views – when newspapers &
television throw at them only processed opinions* (GRANT)

Bombarded by business-as-heroism – we crouch – our ears blown
– or numb

A laugh track has been synchronized to our *lack of transparency*

Mumbling – *once upon a time* – we deny having heard the call to
full surrender

*

I'm not nearly as optimistic as Bron was – those are NAFTA *geese*
I hear

We've changed since she died – our poems have changed

(And yes – change is health – not writing the same poem means
we out-make palaver)

(And yes – process – going-making – is more essential than
product – the little square ones)

When I try to explore how Wallace's voice has evolved – I mean
I wish it could have

Cheap survivor guilt – I know – for getting on with all this slower
dying without her – poems otherwise – muddling through

*

*So the teacher calls up the mother – & the mother says – I couldn't think of
a better pair of names for a couple of bastards*

I always hear that joke told in Bron's voice now – & it makes me
grin

∼

Dubious

A vanishing act – blow the candle out – a calling – *I was here now this is here*

To perform for praise – to get strokes – applause – but the poem drowns in *apple sauce* – lacklustre

At the open mike – a young woman chanting to a humming dildo – young men who need therapy for their misogyny – not praise for their anger

To hear – sprites *&* hooks (islands of repair) – between each syllable – cleanly – without the static of ambition

Hope becomes the expectation of finding next an intricately imperfect process that might prove all of one's own imperfections worthy & irrelevant

To ritualize sharing – the text un-sacred – a reading / a show – not a slide-show of pages

The way Utah Phillips would mix folk songs with Wobbly anecdotes – toward a *Chautauqua* – tales of political betrayal – *as you remember*

He flatters us for knowing more than we do – poses lost history as common sharehold

To step over *Reader & Book* – over *Artist & Model* – over *Patient &
Shrink* – over *Watcher & TV* – over the sustained illusions of one-
on-one

A zone mostly pantheistic – Homer Hollowbone – Dr Fish –
Rumpelstiltskin

Call-backs for the deranged – misanthropic – tea-ballad spinster –
sad-sacks (doubt-riddled – off-key – *hoorah*)

To keep a poem mammal – unreptilian – we are not *machines
to chirp* as Deleuze & Guattari argue – we are organisms – have
minds not mind-sets

Grease-waft – neither ointment nor point – arcane relations
between the Periodic Table & the Alphabet

Even the sacred gills of anonymity – & the penny whistle
maelstrom of the ensemble – can be traps – to concertina absence
– to Breugel the solo

Decadence & sainthood eat from the same bowl – if your food has
been begged for it's bugged

~

77 Florence

Nicky Drumbolis is Arthur Cravan – Art – the man who boxed with
Jack Johnson – then disappeared off Mexico – at sea

Legendary book collector – former & ghost proprietor of *Letters* –
the Toronto bookstore – Queen near Bathurst – small publisher
– same name – various morphs of title

Pedestrian polymath who gives away everything he writes & self-
publishes – everything he publishes lovingly by others

He is house-sitting at his daughter's apartment – near Church &
Wellesley – where a cat needs regular injections

We will pick him up there & return him on time for the next
treatment

A small man – white pony-tail – his face has gotten puffier – he
has a limp these days – as he walks to the car there comes a wince
of pain to his lower back

He stops a moment & mumbles a curse to the pain – Arthur
Cravan – the nephew of Oscar Wilde – the love of Mina Loy's life

As we drive to his warehouse-home – he talks in enthusiastic
lectures – from a seemingly bottomless scholarly catalogue of
research & ephemera

He says he has perfected the skill of reading by osmosis – by simply meditating upon shelves

He has made progress – he admits – from those early Thunder Bay splashed-day-glow coffeehouse years – when Plato (& his whole crew) made no sense at all

Or from Rochdale College in the '60s – where he shared a one bedroom apartment with 13 others

He sees himself back then – wiped on acid – standing naked – frozen – a broom in mid-sweep – *stymied by the dilemma of co-ordinates*

Solving stasis by saying the names – the nouns – Adaming

The Troubadours – the Birth of the Alphabet – Olson & Sauer – the Phoenicians – the Dominicans

Oh – God yes – & – of course – The Unheard-Ofs – those Immortals

Arthur Cravan – who gives out *Pound Notes* at small press fairs – but also collects Red Fisher – the TV poet/fisherman – early 60s

We pull up to his Parkdale warehouse – studio – un-fronted bookstore – warren – office – church

The Dark Lost Library of the Small Press & its Tributaries

A weathered wooden blue door up a metal fire escape shrined
with found metal – driftwood – toys – religious icons

Abandoned palettes from the artist lofts near-by lean in stacks
against the wall – if he ever has to move – but where – where –
these will come in handy

As we enter – starting right at the door – carefully gradated piles
of books – sway – standing free on either side of a deep paper
labyrinth that must be carefully gone along – sideways

Further in – boxes of books – 3-deep – loom – on all sides – to the
high ceiling

There are whole disciplines of research & categories of collecting
that can't be got at right now

Two long glass display tables (from the bookstore days) have been
gradually buried – over – there-abouts

Everywhere – gem-titles are turned face-out on the ranked shelves
for their oddity – beauty – typeface

There are books here so rare – so limited of issue – so localized in
concept – only known extant copies – matchbook one-offs

From a ridgepole hangs – on a black t-shirt – an image of
bpNichol – resident saint – many saints in one – old pal

This is genius – with its head down – disguised as obsession – the obsidian of retail

This is encyclopedic love (contact/use) of/with language/paper/ type/history/ideas/the self – art – craven

We are inside an accordion folio-mind – a black-box theatre-portrait – of itself – a wild gift of curating – curation-creation

This recent April flames engulfed Baghdad's National Library destroying manuscripts untold centuries old

Almost nothing remains of that great library's tens of thousands of manuscripts – books – & Iraqi newspapers

In light of such atrocities – Drumbolis's preservation instinct means – to catch the glowing ashes – & save them – so the world-as-book can be – if not rebuilt – at least remembered – intensely

After years of research – Nicky has – out of a mantra of curses & generosity – grown – written – two monumentally important – anonymous – intimidatingly erudite – copiously footnoted – fat texts

God's Wand (2002) – & *Myth as Math* (2007)

PhDs & Honorary Doctorates have been awarded for much less

These volumes have been given away – officially unnoticed

54

Also published over the years – untold editions & compendiums
by Arthur Cravan & others – little design-wonders – booklets –
books – ephemera

*Telluric & Magnetic: a Sift of Thirteen Poems from the Complete Poetry of
César Vallejo translated by Clayton Eshleman*

Excerpts from *Songs of the Sespe & Other Rhymes* by Frank D Felt

The laurels/are meant/to be carried – /not ridden

77 Florence – where the book trade – & the Age of the Book – &
the Age of Letter Writing – all tank together & thrive

The history of the typed world is being squirreled away – & fought for

Against the heavy smoker in the basement studio – doesn't he
know what smoke can to do books

Against faulty plumbing & rumored plans to convert the
building to condos – 77 Florence – where pilgrims arrive – in
bewilderment

Where a plaque will go – if there is a stand of brick to attach it to
– *Arthur Cravan*

Who might have also been B Traven (hear the rhyme) – author of
The Treasure of the Sierra Madre

At the local roti restaurant – Nicky says – *These people have been feeding me well for eighteen years now*

He talks to the cook through the service window – if the cook will give him a list of titles of books he likes – then Nicky will keep his eye open for them at the university book sales that are coming up

Grizzled faith-keeper – irreverent classicist – Champion of The Eccentrics of Quality

The fires kept alive by Drumbolis – during these bleak & gimmick-bookish times – are rare & miraculous – considering

Poverty – a gift economy – obscurity – pseudonymity – the demise of his storefront

Crankiness – no to government funding – & now – health problems

After an accident – he continues to work as a devil at Coach House Press

Choosing end-page paper – & cutting it just so – for the water-mark to stay revealed – printing – trimming – midwifing folios

We drive up bpNichol Lane – Nicky lets himself in to the legendary squat old press building – (also recently threatened with closure) – after hours – to pick up a fresh copy of his own latest book

Comes out with a fistful of discard copies – recent titles – Nicole
Brossard – gifts – *here*

Fondles – raves about them – their designs – lamenting the
bungled spines

When we drop him off – back at his daughter's place – he is still
talking – promoting the worth of others

Remember Tim Lander from Vancouver Island – who made his
own handwritten books – even handwritten catalogues for them

Art limps across Wellesley – waving back at us

With him go many astounding readers – & forgotten writers –
persisting

Limping – held in fervent trust – as he goes up

To give the cat its hypo

~

Disclosure

Clarity is not pure – it's intricate

As *a terrible beauty is born* (YEATS)

*

Polish poets – Tadeusz Różewicz & Zbigniew Herbert – began again by asking

What of language belongs to us – that isn't ashamed – bloody –
dehumanized – compromised – sold

They gave up on poetry – then built an on-guard music back up from scratch

Różewicz grew a new imagination from one smell (cinnamon)

Herbert invented Mr Cogito because cognition had been so pulverized

*

Rhythm is knowledge

As *a savage servility slides by on grease* (LOWELL)

*

Cahier d'un retour au pays natal (AIMÉ CÉSAIRE, 1938)

André Breton finds a stenciled copy of this defiant French Martinique poem on the counter of a haberdasher's shop in New York in 1940

Return to my Native Land (JOHN BERGER & ANNA BOSTOCK, translators, 1969)

*

To be a *terroir*-ist – so locally quirk-private – your *truthishness* is incomprehensibly exact (see CHAR or CELAN)

The hornpipe of a home-scar – a rage-harvest (ballad)

*

Error is character

As *they feed they lion & he come* (LEVINE)

*

George Oppen says prosody is not *how to write poetry* – but how to write *the poem in front of you*

Prosody carries the relation of things & the sequence

The instant of meaning – the achievement of meaning & presence – the sequence of disclosure

Not simply the stone *say* – or the sung *it*

But the artisanry of focusing simultaneously on signs & coordinating sounds – while underway – in *this* poem right here – theory-less

A shuttlecock page-floor *how-to* that accrues – choreographed syllables – in the instances of their approximations

*

The poem about me as a boy shooting the dog when my dad told me to

Didn't ring clear in its flaw-rhythms – until I scraped down to the rage-line

Nothing but nothing would be beneath me (MCHUGH)

*

I should have shot my father

⁓

She Loved the Ocean

Summer 1992 – Libby Scheier & I drive to New York together for
a holiday

To visit her old neighbourhood – & to face down the basement
where she had been abused as a child

*

Crouching was my idea

To scrunch down as small as she was back then – & Libby's
therapist said (later) yes that might have helped the memories
come back

I took some photos – they are dark – we look startled

We look as if we are tunnelling through thick churned-up brown
paint

We are murky figures leaning away from ruthlessness – as in
paintings by Soutine

We are in that basement in Brooklyn – under the apartment
building where Libby grew up – near the school Woody Allen
went to

A warm grease-pit smell – *small town garages my father worked in*

Saturday afternoons – me bored & alone in the Pontiac up on the hoist

*Watching the men drink & laugh below – I still remember a few of the
dirty jokes they told – they would forget I was up there*

*If you're not doing anything young man says the cop get out here & hold
the flashlight*

Enough of what had happened to Libby had happened to me too

I felt frightened down there with her – eager to get the pilgrimage
over – & go drink

*

The quad at the side of the building was piled with garbage – the
Super – suspicious – had let us go down there for fifteen minutes
– for free

She didn't know that in each breast pocket Libby had an
American fifty – crisp & ready

They had all been playing when the older boy grabbed her &
dragged her in there & did it

After being forced to her knees – she remembered nothing

The memory had crawled out of her brain – hidden in her
muscles & bones

Crouching might have been too submissive a posture – probably
just as well I didn't think to suggest that until after

*

Then we went & found a pastry shop that sold Charlotte Russes
– angel food cakes in paper cups – you push up the detached
bottom

Libby got some cream on those purple elephants parading across
the pockets of her loose silk shirt – the whipped cream soaked
through the elephants & dampened the money

The Charlotte Russes were not as tasty as she remembered them
being – but not bad for sugared air – not an everyday thing

Sexy treats – I suppose – with all that cream – & the cherry on top
– its little stem rising in a gentle curve – flaring slightly at its tip

Reaching for its tree – the grasping nostril of a tiny elephant's
trunk

*

There were Haitians playing cards on a milk crate under the
overpass

A petite yellow knot of a woman outside the pastry shop confided in us about the state of the neighbourhood

Prognosis – influx of the wrong blood – decorum all shot to hell – & kissed goodbye with a Hebrew epithet

Then we drove back out to Long Island – Bayshore – where we were staying – in a motel beside a strip-mall

The World's Best Bagel Factory – & two package liquor stores

*

There were a few abandoned zones in the middle rush of the freeway lanes

Dead going-concerns – where I would have liked to get out – with my headache

Gasless islands of orange mesh – on which life is an un-killable weed – passed at 80 mph – constantly

*

When we got back to our room – to air conditioning – there were the two twenty-six ounce bottles of *Teachers* scotch I had bought – I got ice

Also – under the sink in the bathroom – lodged in the bend of

66

the pipe – I had hidden two quart bottles of pre-made vodka
cocktail – blackberry & peach – one from each package store

The lids screwed off to become collectable cups – & it was
pleasant sitting on the tiles – listening to the little stink-fan in the
ceiling – while Libby slept

The plan was to spend a few days on Fire Island before we drove
back to Toronto

This was Libby's second visit to the courtyard/basement – & she
said she would probably return to it again

I'm not that way about what happened to me

Like the nodding weeds on those turnpike islands – in those
days I stopped just short of dying – & then waited to see what
happened next

*

I sure loved Fire Island though

The sand was black under its tan – purple under its black – & grey
under its purple – as my feet sank deeper into the undertow

I saw Libby far along the beach – half-obscured by fog – we looked
toward each other at the same moment

We waved to each other – & then both turned away – she loved
the ocean

*

At lunch – hurricane warnings – rain came before our scrod

We helped hook down the restaurant's green screens – & then
drank at the bar & watched the storm come in

On the jukebox I played *Better Class of Loser* by Randy Travis –
true son of George Jones – & we talked about *Key Largo* – Lionel
Barrymore in a wheelchair by then

*

Her abuser – she said – lived in Florida – had a wife & kids

She had tracked him down – & then not known what to do to get
revenge

Had felt worse to know where he was – couldn't stop imagining
him with his daughters

After the storm cleared – we moved out onto the patio – ordered
Irish coffees – & then double slings

Libby was talking about renting a beach house next summer – we
could bring our kids – she had noticed a rental number tacked on
a gate at the other shore

I walked back by myself to the beach to copy down the number

Lightly drunk – glazed – I drifted between deceptively humble villas obscured by bamboo landscaping

*

A doe & a fawn were grazing in a yard – oblivious – heads down – nibbling

I stopped – held my breath – they came right up to me

The fawn's spots may have been sun-dapple – its muzzle was sweating

The fawn nuzzled the doe – wiping grass-flecked slobber along her withers

The doe snorted – regaled her head high – smelling me

Inches away now – she swung – & the fawn swung as its mother's shadow

They bolted into the dry scrub as one – & me as one with them

Wrenching the last grain of me free from that tarred basement in Brooklyn

*

I brought back the number – but it was over between us

Libby had felt the beach moment give way too

She knew that I would not stay in the filth of the quad to protect her

Pathetic at trust – we bullied from each other what final affections we got

Two crouchers

~

The Small Sacrifice

Let's be honest – we're just talking here

The straight goods – the hard truth – the simple isolated story – the way it is – just the facts – let's be blunt – no bull

What you are about to hear will not be polite – it will startle you out of your complacencies – it will be good for you – trust us – loosen up

*

We all recognize this stance & pitch – we're all guilty of having used it

Irving Layton – for one – promoted himself this way – in his lesser poems that show such contempt for the rich women of Westmount

They are frigid & he is their Messiah – they are stupid about art & he is their satyr-professor

*

You will remember how the back covers of poetry books by academics used to brag a list of the humblest jobs – *worm picker/ Department Chair*

I used to cheer the worm in the Chair – saw virtue in the blunt

I said – *invented lives are insults to our life stories* – oh I wanted to be real & believe in myself as folk

To make progress happen by calling poems tools

I don't believe in myself that much anymore – or progress – but I believe in my poems more than I used to

They still pick worms – but have made up their own silly dances

They seem more political somehow – as they widen – & reach compulsively – with reverence – into the intricate & democratic decorum of sound

To invite texture not topic

*

When Layton says – in the last line of *The Bull Calf* – *I turned away and wept*

He is flaunting an emotional – sexual – poetic – & political superiority

He is pointing to his own larger – freer – feeling – the line is theatre – not truth

We may think we have broken through the sentimental – into a raw & beautiful truth

The unsayable zinger feels like health – transgression is vitalizing

Startling – quotable – epigraphic – but the truth is always more complicated

Or sight-to-the-blind simple – as in Basho

Plop – or *cow plop*

*

Beware studied innocence too

(The perpetually zany teenager-voice of the small press mogul in his 50s)

Blake's *Songs of Innocence* – are Sunday school lessons

But in his *Introduction* – Blake says – *And I made a rural pen/And I stain'd the water clear*

Simplicity & clarity are linked always by active accident to surprise – not to any plan or pose

Where the Blues is not a kit – where Basho's heart – startled – leaps *as* frog – *with* frog

Where action is compulsion without institution – not charity – or advice – or imitation

Where the simply-stated is an urge – a jerk-response – not a thought – or a technique

There – or there abouts

*

Viscerally – there are blunt subjects that bother me – we have a history – certain crudities & I

Critically – it is not a *subject* – but a *method* that bothers me – the *implications behind* certain methods (& their forms)

Subject – *choosing* a subject – can be a way to lie about complexity

To not use *sincerity* as a technique to advertise or preach

(*Tristram Shandy* is more humane than any anthem)

*

There are many ways to enact sincerity

If a poem is not in your face – if it is not *slammed* into your face – it is not necessarily behind your back

If a poem is long or complicated – not readily gotten – un-
gettable even – it is not necessarily two-faced

*

Here's what Octavio Paz says about Pop

*Unlike Dada & Surrealism – Pop Art from the beginning was
a tributary of the industrial current – a small stream feeding into
the system of circulation of objects*

*Its products are not defiant challenges of the museum or rejections of
the consumers' aesthetic that characterizes our time – they are consumer
products*

*Far from being a criticism of the marketplace – this art is one of its
manifestations – a mannequin rather than a true apparition*

*

Robert Frost is now a Colonel Sanders figure – a couple of his
lines survive as bites

Even *Howl* is a stuffed red wheelbarrow toy – this is what Nicole
Brossard & Robin Blaser mean to avoid by making poems so wilily

To revive words from their scab hollowness – to repeat words until
their labia-gills reconstitute

*

Or George Orwell – 1946 – *Politics & the English Language*

English – he says – has gotten clogged by fluff – unconsidered
phrases come forth as high falderal – in verse – in prose – in news

Orwell was convinced that no-nonsense sentences could fix all
gobbledygook

They can't – Plain English is now just another propaganda-
costume

*

The epigraph & the idiom (*a bean in the ear/he who*)

The avuncularity of these little flat narration-kits

Edible rulers

*

In the late '70s – when the politicians in Ottawa found out that
bill bissett was getting Canada Council money to type 3 letters –
C-U-M – onto a page into the shape of an erect penis

There was a petty uproar in the House – bill got mentioned
during Discussion Period – how dare words draw *carnivale*

76

How dare bissett invoke by generous courage (for years/for ears)
his blazing indictments of

His outright dismissal by galaxy-wide acceptance of – every
politician's right-angled mendacity

And of every little poem that brags righteous feeling – when it
says some version of – *my daughter is sleeping/on Christmas Eve/as I
remember/Pindar*

*

Or consider my old friend Dan Jones – whose suicide – at least in
part – had something to do with the failure of literary ambition

Jones – whose most famous poem is crude/surreal & child-like
(pagan) – *Things I Have Put Into My Asshole*

Saliva & semen & butter & baby oil,
tongues & thumbs & fingers of women,
the cock of an old man,
the cock of a Mexican boy,
the cock of my sister's boyfriend,
my hand,
candles & felt marking pens,
cucumbers & carrots,
Sandra's mother's vibrator,
the intersection of Bathurst & Queen,
Honest Ed's Warehouse,
Hamilton Ontario,

& just today the CN Tower:
I came all over Bay Street,
as the world's highest disco
rotated upon my prostate.
YOU ARE FREE NOW TORONTONIANS!
It lies limp on the frozen surface
of Lake Ontario.
You can barely see the tungsten bulbs
through the film of K-Y jelly.
GO FREE TORONTONIANS!
The small sacrifice
of a very large asshole.

*

A crowd-pleaser – the list – elemental in its procedures

Though it be up in arms (as above) – as a form the list is always in
uniform

Its accumulativeness resists rebellion like a Boy Scout campfire –
its military rhythms endorse easy listening

*

Our sometimes worthy impulse to shock & say the unadorned –
can become aligned – by form alone – with art that is too careful

Too accurate – too simple – too *good* – in a school-bookish or
mechanized way

The blunt & *the correct* can end up using the same *Rules of Order*

See *The Captive Mind* (1953) – in which Czesław Miłosz chronicles
the gradual corruption of the minds of artists by totalitarianism in
central Europe

You start speaking out – & end up speaking for – or not at all

*

It's Not Acceptable to be Fatso – says Aase Berg

*I hope for poetic expressions that are aggressive – baroque & esoteric – I
prefer ridiculous & embarrassing to perfection*

*On the literary market – which is dominated by the aesthetic & social
ideals of the upper middle class – it is unacceptable to be excessive in any
way – one adjective too many & you're out*

*There's a stubborn cliché that the sober – quiet & elegant – the so-called –
simple is categorically more informative than the noisy*

*The fleshy – screamy & overdone – the vulgar – desperate & pathetic are
so taboo in our culture*

*

The writing factories have turned Orwell's warning into a doctrine
of propriety

The mood-drenched simple ending (*I turned away and wept*) has
become a law of closure – a truth-mask

*

The small sacrifice – of Jones's poem – is a giant sexual fantasy –
the Colossus as Liberator

The only desk-sacrifice a writer can make is patience & silence &
focus

The invited maybe comes – *defiance* spelled *evidence* – *quiet* never
quite spelling *quit*

*

Innocence is lightning – it has no mood except surprise

It can be invited but not built – it stops blog-wallow cold

The manufacture of innocence is a drawing of a light bulb

We have been taught to read as light the straight lines coming
from the icon

*

In *The Other Voice* Paz (again) says

*If a new form of political thought were to emerge – the influence of poetry would
be indirect – reminding us of certain buried realities – restoring them to life
– preserving them*

*Poetry can respond in no other way – its influence must be indirect –
intimidating – suggesting – inspiring*

*

The subverting of syntactical structures is an *indirect* version of
what students did in Paris in '68

They made the thoroughfares impassable so that dialogue would
have to be re-invented – revitalized – *across* the class lines

Diagonal Man – says an old Bread & Puppet poster

*

My other guiding critics – in this circling outward away from the
blunt – are Guy Davenport & Edmund Jabès

Davenport explains how *Every Force Evolves A Form* – his verb carefully chosen

The evolving force – or Olson's *Push* (again) – or Lorca's *Duende* – or what I call *compulsion*

What – *seems to insist upon* – being written

*

Another title – Jabès's *The Little Book of Unsuspected Subversion*

To proceed by gathering into curio-cabinets various samples *that seem to* relate

Beyond surprise & repetition – everything seeks everything

*

So – Paz's word *indirection* – Davenport's word *evolve* – & Jabès's phrase *unsuspected subversion*

The indirect evolving of unsuspected subversion

A counter to Punk & Pop & The New Work Writing & People's Poetry *etc*

Bluntness (agenda) stunts discovery (addenda)

*

It is just not so simple – or as noble – as crying when the calf dies
– never has been – never will be

To establish room – plus legitimacy – for voice – among the
corrupt middle

By leaping *sidelong* head-last into the dark disorientations of *woids*

*

A circle's line is not composed of dots – my dash is not a series of
periods

Though I like the word *spleen* – I do not believe the tale that says I
have one

*

As I listen for the ajar to pulse – I am awakened not by topics –
but by typos

A period in a list of commas – a *though* that was meant to be
thought

That period among commas – is a flaw among flow – & where
though has been set as *thought* – I hear a ripe hesitation – instead
of knowing

A hesitant *though* is inside *thought* – it has been there this whole time

Play – or the full Golem

*

An analogy – the old dog is sleeping on the porch

You watch the dog through the screen-door – you have to put the dog down – you write a song called *Old Shep*

The door is locked – you cannot see the dog except through the screen – which is language

Realizing this – you begin to notice the screen – not the dog

Soon you see only the screen – so you write a book called *Screens*

What a word refers to is another word (PAZ)

Now the dog gets up & comes through a little door in the door – a little trap you hadn't noticed before – *What*

Old Shep is all covered with ads & slogans like a telecast – he is rubbing projected sub-heads up against you – *What*

This is a new kind of dog – maybe it's not even a dog anymore

Maybe you won't have to put it down

*

Against this analogy – the false politics of honesty

Layton's line about the calf – my own line (*I should have shot my father*)

The thousands of poems that get pared down to thin polite columns of memory in writing workshops every summer

An industry of domestic *enjambment* – denial or dismissal of the screen in the door

*

Realism – is a useful falsehood – a tear-jerker

But when it is waved as part of a campaign to dummy-down the complexity of impression/expression

Realism (*saliva & semen & butter & baby oil*) becomes emotional Fascism

If Dan Jones could have crawled past blunt confessional Punk animations – he might still be alive

He might have become our Lorca – *nieve nardo y salina*

*

We're just talking here

As the paws fall off the story & are replaced by pauses that
fall off

As frost keeps carving its Urdu in the asphalt

∼

The Bad Sequence

This is a bad sequence

The bad sequence is ready for its interview about line one

The bad sequence is a school project with a moustache

The bad sequence is an incomprehensible tag – name as spoor –
on every garage door along the alley – *incomprehensile*

The bad sequence is a gloating of bones – a parade of structure –
the skeleton t-shirt

The bad sequence knew where it was going before it went – then
got the grant to go – but had already gone by applying – it is a
chronicle of the application as journey

The bad sequence is a preached-over dry-spell

The bad sequence's subject is both armour & amour – sloshed
in a suit of beer cans it withholds forth – beseechingly – a spill of
clanking

The bad sequence is overly sub-title proud

The bad sequence knows that the self-sufficient line does not a
book make

When the bad sequence swears – its blasphemies sound virginal –
as if chosen with tweezers

The bad sequence is a cut-&-past job

The bad sequence carries its wedding dress from door-to-door –
selling light bulbs

The bad sequence has chosen erudite funny & campy quotes as
epigraphs to suggest that it is erudite funny campy – this is like
sticking your head through a hole in a painted wall at a carnival
so that in the resultant photograph it looks as if you were having
tea with the Queen

The bad sequence has been too busy waiting for the mailman to
water its plants

The bad sequence has read something you haven't – & in that
advantage mistakenly hears poetry

The bad sequence eats its bronzed booties – (not really – an
exaggerated mime of eating its bronzed booties – they are up its
sleeve)

The bad sequence will not stop until it has completed one section
about every card in a tarot deck made of dried banana leaves – or
every country no longer found on maps (ignore why) – or every
private letter found by helicopter-light behind a wall – or every
organ in the body (& then some – *a poem for voices*)

(Who gives a good god)

In a bad sequence it is usually easy to tell which poem is the
mother-poem – it may appear anywhere in the sequence – but
usually it was the first one written – look for the only self-
contained section – the one all the others feed (or play) off of –
sometimes it is a real poem – or was before it began to diversify its
holdings

The bad sequence's mother is the Canada Council for the Arts
– she sings to the child in the womb a song of research & travel
grants – prospectuses – itineraries

Its father teaches a graduate poetry workshop – his favourite
saying is *only connect*

The stations of the cross will get a grant – but prayer will not

Topical & wrenching ruminations upon an ancestor's thimble collection
– or a trek to Tuck-Your-Shirt-In – these are Mother's ideals of
poetry

Each year Father bestows MAs for bad sequences on budding
novelists

Or the bad sequence tries to glorify all that is ironically wacko –
raspberry bloop forget it next huh sheesh git

Catch-all – *Chicken Little/peanut brittle – Palaver & Cash: attorneys
at law*

(The smirk on the drone – the sarcasm of the bore – these are their red noses)

The bad sequence calls a rooster's comb its *brainglove* – a chicken's wattles its *voicehammock*

The bad sequence makes driftwood wear a cap-&-gown

(Why have writing's drawing-roots been severed)

The bad sequence doesn't know when to quit – it milks the ovation

If poets clap for themselves – so what – only pets get enough attention

But then who claps for the reader

How grandiose *trilogy* sounds when craned-in to a small site like poetry – the hands are in confusion – but the blueprints are already selling the loft condos

The bad sequence is so fully realized – don't you just want to smash it – interrupt its completion – direction

The bad sequence deletes its distractions

The bad sequence is a *Find Waldo* book – *Find Walden* – *Find Waldorf*

Priests are torturing The Good Sequence – apparently there
are laws against removing the ghosts of history & story from
dictionaries – meanwhile Sunlight's unflappable surrealism
measures & swabs the room

Leave the words alone – they are not re-enactments

The bad sequence thinks that what it hasn't read is a travesty

The bad sequence wants the reader to give it magic beans for
its little feverish sacred cow – but *its* beans should offer magic to
make un-sacred *our* cows

The bad sequence – if flattered – embarrasses everyone by starting
to tell jokes in dialect

The bad sequence's randomness is on a loop: *peek-a-boo* (*surprise*) –
yoo-hoo (*surprise*) – (the toy's precociousness was maddening – we
took the batteries out but it still wouldn't shut up – so we banished
it to the porch where it kept peek-a-booing no one until it froze)

Echo is not structure – it is structure hitting a wall

The easy beauty of the idea of writing a serial poem is a lie

Unwrenched blurts bore – *hand over the blurt-wrench – Alphy*

To extrapolate is to capitalize – profit & personify – sections are
characters

The bad sequence cannot be unentitied or strobeless

The bad sequence implies that its hands are besmirched by
islands of Quink – foxholes of tinkering – agonized-over periods
(as if they were locations on maps)

But listen closely – hear keys percolating – that water-boiling
sound is unmistakably clean – the Munroe Doctrine morphed
galactic

The bad sequence has a vague sense that to play with words is
ultra modern – *bed sea quench*

How does the seabed quench its thirst – thought Bad Sequence – & was
very pleased with itself for thinking so – it would run down to the
garden & tell Farmer Granting-Officer right away

Time is what the bad sequence needs – Galapagos & Blurt – but
not News

In Galapagos poems & Blurt poems *thought* can hold *awe* – *Thawet*

But News poems are only advertisements for Time –
commentaries on Time – doctored photos of Time crying

The bad sequence can't (blurt) sneeze – it is on anti-what-history-
means (antihistamines)

So the bad sequence needs time as tinkerer/pickler/weatherer

Think of Joseph Cornell baking painted boards in his kitchen
oven to get just the right pattern of cracks in the old paint – those
cracks in one of his art boxes now – eloquent as dream-scripts –
eloquent as The Accidental

The unfinished poem – face-down on the floor – under the desk
– for months – is not really waiting – it doesn't care – when it gets
the word it needs – then it will care

Time as Stanley Kunitz – *the bud of the flower at first will not be
distinguishable from the head of the snake*

Time as Probation Officer – *this is not about something the poem
needs to have happen to it – this is about something that you need to have
happen to you*

*Wait – watch the hills or hike alone through them – after the baby is born –
or your bifocals are stepped on – the word the poem needs might be there in
an anchored way it never could have been before*

But the bad sequence hears – *Baby Moses among the rushes* – &
thinks – *Moses during rush hour*

The bad sequence needs to stop seeing the † & the *I* & the *me*
in *Time*

Poor Bad Sequence doesn't know that sometimes a poem just
happens to a person like a long illness

The old board baking in the oven smells so much like a horse &
buggy it clomps

Alignments of patience are almost whistling

The word may not be worth the wait, but the wait will be worth
the word

Hey – Bad Sequence – the recipe is not one of the ingredients

At its best the bad sequence replaces cleverness with compulsion –
chases intricacies of meaning with scraps of song

The bad sequence can't help it – or can it – half of the book's
budget will be spent on the colour cover – the biggest editing
concern will be choice of font – *standard format may dictate final
content* – *no problemo*

(*Deadlines* is such an ominous word when publishing poetry)

The bad sequence is discouraged – why shouldn't it be – it is not
hardcover – nor is its author – pudding where an exoskeleton
should be – words one steps in

Couldn't all the parts be melted together to make something
smaller but more interesting or more complicated

Whoosh – smear – squelch – anti-tick-tick – unhoodwinkable

94

The bad sequence's career is not on the line – each book is
another title in the bag

The economics of acknowledgements – thanks to everyone & we
do mean everyone

This is the old subscribers game from the Eighteenth Century
– this is how *Stringband* financed its third album *Thanks To The
Following* in 1977 by filling the back cover with the names of those
who had sent in money – Bronwen Wallace & Ron Baxter of
Windsor (then) among them

The bad sequence is an enlisted list – the drift regimented – a
laugh track & orders

The bad sequence finds double meanings everywhere – it
ridicules the archaic – it pokes fun at people's names –
W A Stead – get it

This is Adam – the Father of Namers – smirking like Don Rickles

The bad sequence is a cold joke

To tell a literary anecdote – the bad sequence puts on its shit-
eating-grin mask

Carl Sandburg's lie is that The Simple are simple – Lorine
Niedecker's truth is that Complexity can be a local god

Complexity as craft show kitchen-witch

The bad sequence is also reactionary when it comes to the spiritual – though lightning strike the pen-hand with sulfurous quills & feathers – writing must be gravity – otherwise how could the ancient columns continue to *tsk tsk* – where might all the dark ATM slots lead

I is ranting – *I wrote I said I need to I am that undiscovered continent that I must believe I mean I want to I am that tiny island of what I know I have not lost I am desperate for A to reach B before it has reached A*

Bad Sequence says – *I understand completely – it must be so difficult for you – do you mind if I write down what you just said – did you say* tiny island – *perhaps* rocky nub – the rocky nub of what I know – *sounds better – good – that's very good – & interesting – it reminds me of*

Turn a light off by forgetting about it – turn it back on by remembering

Poetry – a light – silence turns off & on – by forgetting & remembering

As we try to hear – & not hear – silence's hum

The bad sequence isn't so bad

Who cares – it's not evil

⌒

A Thin Plea

Our national bird – for years – was – as A M Klein said –
the rocking chair

I don't know what our national bird is now – but my totem bird is
the killdeer

Its names – odd mannerisms – & cry – explain bits about me – in
riddles

My daily writing self at 57 has accrued the usual odd habits &
noises – there are awful names I know myself by – lie-dances I
perform

In my hopelessness I half-hope my deflections might honour me

In open fields my bird ranges – it nests near cow plops & hooves –
its only protection a desperate busking

If a person or a creature approaches its eggs – the killdeer
pretends to have a broken wing – it flits near – then hovers away
– one wing splints forward at an unnatural angle – its cry seems so
plaintive

Intruders are diverted from its eggs by a chance at catching the
adult

97

Like that wounded arrow-maker – Philoctetes – I have a broken wing – of sorts

Something wrong with my hands – eczema – nerves

My palms – red & dry – split along their lifelines – & bleed

It is difficult to wear white shirts – for instance

When I fall asleep I always go right back to the same fields I grew up in

Dreaming – I wander in those fields – my hands bleed into the furrows – I look for my eggs – I cry

I am not lying – but there has always been a hint of puppetry to my whining

I grew up on farms between Bobcaygeon & Fenelon Falls – mid-century – mid-Ontario – between Reaney's townships to the southwest – & Purdy's country slightly north to the east

When I write I am always mid-field – on one leg – the other poised over killdeer eggs

Have almost stepped on them again – but I hold the pose & write instead

Around me the bird cries its lies – as I hover there – pen poised

I am overcome & rejuvenated by imbalance – complexity

Its Latin name is *Charadrius vociferus* – a vociferous charade – its
common name – *killdeer* – is a yoking of *precious* & *doomed*

*

Though you'd never know it to look here – I don't like to talk
about writing – I always feel as if I am about to get slapped for
showing off

My writing has been more about my life than my life has been
about writing – the goal always better balance – a safer self –
poetry has so little to do with writing

I'd rather talk about how you got your car started that cold
morning – or about *your* writing – if you insist

I don't know where my eggs are – or what I am still so guarded
about – or whether I even have any eggs still intact

I have hidden my poems in stumps – under floorboards – behind
pseudonyms – in other people's books – in bus station lockers –
under bridges – down my pants – & in my mouth

Like Yannis Ritsos I have put poems in jars & buried them on
islands in Greece

I have put my poems in a Crown Royal bag – tied a length of
binder twine to the bag's yellow cord – & then lowered the lot
down a groundhog hole

99

Where the audacity to publish comes from – I don't want to know

Oddly – confession has figured in my writing – I have populated my poems with real people who would resent my use of them if they knew

I have operated on myself in public – I have abused language because I was abused

It's not true that I have saved my life by writing (though I often say so)

But I have – like the killdeer – made vaudeville of my pain – to distract my enemies – & this has distracted me too

I have hidden myself by pointing at myself – when the poems seem to point at actual scabs – they are pointing away

Coming from a bookless home – I have never gotten over an innate suspicion of text – even my own

I am being as honest as I can – though the hand itself is a puppet – a naked puppet

Give a pen to a naked puppet & ask it to write – in this case – the truth

In my case – you get an approximation of the killdeer – the pen is the beak

My pain – my pain – at first I thought that was what poets said

My pain – my pain – eventually I wanted not to mean it – now
sometimes I don't mean it – but I say it anyway

*

Killdeer – there isn't much to say – just *here I am here I am*

Another waving of old tools as if they were broken wings

A thin plea *my pain my pain* – lies dying out in the dry grass – dying
out in starlessness

A few small poems have stayed warm

*

My pain – my pain – I need a new bird – that will eat the old one

If I put cream on my hands each day – the holes close up

Years of not drinking – years of therapy – the gold thread of a
third marriage – the inflatable anchorage of my children – these
have healed me – not *cleverness* or *career* or *language*

What if all I know how to write is a cry – what if health has no
poem – where are those goading – imaginary – enemies when
I need them

*

Carl Jung said our great endeavour is to transfer the centre from ego to Self – capital S – this is what Killdeer has been up to – falsehood-altruism

My *IIIII*s are too close together

I have come to trust choruses & group photos more than solos & head-shots

I would prepare my poems for a time when I won't be around to wave my cap to keep the flies off them

A poem – like a life – begins in ego – but it needs to move its centre to the Self

By this I do not mean that a poem should address universal themes – God no

I mean – cut the first person pronoun adrift – & the lyric will give up its addiction to pain

It may still be talking about pain – but it will have begun to circle – dithyrambic – in a field you are only one aspect of

Eventually the poem will ask you to give it away – like a bride – to its own imbalance & complexity

You will remember that *anon* has two meanings – nameless – & soon – getting out from under a name takes patience

*

When I can't sleep – when I'm sick – when no one else is home –
when I'm lost in transit – I *tinker*

This is my word for what I do – a slow – un-clever – tactile – cheap
– harmless rearranging of odd bits of my nature & gatherings –
until they sing – off-key

I tinker at long sequences – & stay close to notebooks – mostly
when no one is looking

Am increasingly filled with hopelessness – but sometimes when
I'm up to my elbows in a line's perplexities

Confidence lands its flocks upon me & I feel – inside the poem –
unafraid

*

Killdeer on my oozing stumps has drummed her wings long & hard

Whipped the years' butcher block rings to crèche shavings –
beaten nests of feathered chips by simulated soar – folded herself
into my pages boatingly

Her desperate ruse has settled into gunwales – her closed cry a
prow's nib

The stumps' roots I thought destined to be fences – are a mob of
keels righting little brown-speckled eggs

Safe – adrift – hoving-to – as cloud-shadow swamps fields

The age of flight is followed by the age of sail

*

A new totem bird & I are just getting to know each other – it is
eating Killdeer slowly

Safer – healthier – silent – I sit in our rocking chair

Maybe I'll tell you what the new bird is called when I know

~

Praxia

Before my daughter was born – I made up this whole legend about her

She would lead a band of women resistance fighters – dressed in furs they would roar across the tundra – on flame-throwing snowmobiles

Hoda – that was her pre-birth name – Hoda would swoop down from the far north – sabotage Yankee strong-holds

Force the damn Americans out of Canada

*

When she was 4-months-old – we moved to Greece – & lived on Crete at first – near Agios Nikolaos

In the 1940s – villagers had been massacred by the occupying Nazis – the cathedral had been partially burned – its orthodox icons darkened by char

I was there – writing on an old door propped between rocks under a fig tree – because I admired those people who had fought so intractably for their island back – in ways my own country never would

On the beach – hidden among reeds – I discovered a German machine-gun bunker – gunless – of crude cement – built to guard the harbour – & still there in 1989

I would crawl in – like a young German – & watch the ancient water through the gun-slot

*

In February – even while the African sun glared – a downpour & double rainbows along the far ridge of the village

Mornings – while we bathed the baby in the sink (in warm rain water from a tank on the roof) – our landlady's knock at the hot shuttered window – an omelette for us – a French fry omelette

Brett Brett – but she thought the baby's name was *Bread* – so she called her the Greek word for bread – ψωμί (psomi)

And *we* thought that our landlady's name – Praxia – meant Peace – but it means Action

*

Lady Brett – Ashley – in Hemingway's *The Sun Also Rises*

That's who we were thinking of – a composite with a snoot-full of problems of her own

We forgot about Brett Hull – the hockey player – son of Bobby

For years Brett gets teased for having a boy's name – for being the young sports star

When she's grown – she legally adds an *e* to her first name – makes it obviously a young woman's name

By one letter – the absurdity of *Stick-Handling in Pamplona* vanishes

*

Twenty years – the vigilante snowmobiles have grown fainter

On bad days I struggle to convince myself that by merely living as best we could we did anything to improve anything

But then I remember how – when Brette's mom was pregnant with her – & working as a counsellor at the Morgentaler Clinic in Toronto

Those rabid Fascists with their foetus-posters would scream atrocities at her

As she rode by – beamingly healthy to term – standing heavily to peddle her purple bicycle through them

*

I played table tennis with Morgentaler

That would make a fine title for a kid's book – *Playing Table Tennis With Morgentaler*

He was very good

*

Also – there was a Sri Lankan woman – on strike at a mushroom farm – in Surrey BC – in the early '8os

By the picket-line – as I held the flashlight in the dark trailer – she wrote on my chapati with a marker

The word for *union* in Urdu – & I ate it

*

I used to say – *Retsina is what the gods drink when they can afford it* – that meat-freezer-cold pine tang numbing all doubt

The next right thing that makes no sense

I'd take the bus up the cliff from the beach in the morning while Jane & the baby were still asleep

I'd wait in the shade of the square in Zagora for the bakery to open

The next right thing that makes no sense at the time

I'd stumble down through kiwi terraces into the blinding blue of
the Aegean

The day's bread a long hot scar against me

Praying to a swallow of light

*

Sloppiness as libation

Sometimes Brette still gets called *Psomi*

~

Verulam

I long to sail away – always have – grew up to run off – & come back

Now I am trying to grow down – to reluctantly accept my region – my wherewithal as a township

*

When I was born – my parents signed the origin-box on my birth-form – by writing the names of their townships – *Harvey* – *Verulam*

Adjoining backwaters in Victoria County – Ontario

The civil servant who processed that form – crossed out both townships – & wrote *Canadian* over top

Which is sort of a lie – the nation being one thing/stomping grounds another

My folks suffered unflung lives – Cec drove truck – saw Manitoulin Island – Cobalt

The furthest Dot ever traveled from Bobcaygeon – was to Fantasy Gardens in London Ontario

*

Local is my most shameful pride – *local* is what threatened me with
silence

*

The rock-cuts along #7 highway – the sheer red ridges up the
Galway Rd toward Bancroft – their dynamited fossils – vibrate in me

My grandfather – when he wasn't drunk – worked with a
wheelbarrow – hauling limestone slag away after blasting

My father – when he wasn't drunk – drove a Euclid – a Yuke –
hauling granite boulders seamed with quartz

By their labour – I find clear passage – driving north

In those parting waves of rock – I see ancient brows & jaws –
shades that thrust in profile – umber juttings – ancestors

*

My dad – in his cups – would claim he was part Native

He used to bootleg to the Indians at Curve Lake on Saturday
nights when they had their big dances

Before he started the family I grew up in – he had an earlier son
with a Native woman from Curve Lake

That son – Jim – would be 75 or so now

*

We weren't farmers – shopkeepers – or church-goers

Had no land – no god – no business – no business being there

My father was itinerate – truck driver / construction worker /
mechanic / fence builder – munitions factory worker until he lost
part of a finger

Soldier until he broke his leg in seven places in a drunken brawl
in Kingston – & so – to his great shame – never got overseas

*

I live a song & a half south of Perth now – within three hours of
where I'm from – fearing the proximity

But I drive between the rock cuts – & feel at home

*

Less what you say / some days, than / where you say it
(MERRILL GILFILLAN)

*

As a boy – I would look out at the hard-scrabble settlements going by

I'd have my thumb in my mouth – I'd be holding a copy of
Treasure Island

I'd think – *the dullest place to be born – the most boring trees*

I wanted palms & grottos – giraffes – in igloos – I still do

*

But my bird is the killdeer – my colours/grey & green – colours to
hide among

My stone/ limestone – my tree/the hawthorn

My flower/the red trillium – not real red – russet – the shade of
brown that leaks from wet rusted nails

*

Lying on my back – in my log cabin – reading

I study the square beams in the roof – am looking at cuts swung
by lumberjacks – around 1850

I can hear each chop – splintering wood-chips – flying

*

The furthest I ever ran away – was from what my childhood &
region seemed to insist on

Silence – ignorance – bitterness – crudity – xenophobia –
contempt for all that is fanciful (books *etc*) – addiction – violence
– mysogeny

*

When I sing – I cry like the killdeer

In sleep – I fly low over the old farms we didn't own

My cry – this habit – this lie

A home-hum – longing to die – far away – Crete

*

Fling my ashes into that white-eating blue

I will join the faces in the rock-cuts

∼

Envoi

Some trust imagination in the round

I love a wild fountain's clear gush in a gully in a squall
 secreted within its headlands my caress

if this tiny despair-basket I lead with were real
 it would be of woven willow

going is what I trust/in a way

Notes

Daniel Jones (1959–1994)

Margaret Laurence (1926–1987)

Libby Scheier (1946–2000)

Bronwen Wallace (1945–1989)

*

Whenever I travel Greece wounds me – GEORGE SEFERIS

Envoi – after René Char's "La Compagne du Vannier"

*

This book is for Stan Dragland.

*And we have made a station of the way to the hidden city / in the rooms
where we are* – ROBERT DUNCAN

*

"Adios Polka" first appeared in *Dandelion*.

An earlier version of "A Thin Plea" was titled "Killdeer" & appeared in *Event* magazine.

Earlier versions of "The Bad Sequence" appeared as a chapbook with that title from BookThug, 2004, revised in a second edition 2007.

"Dubious" appeared in a looser, longer form on the Griffin Poetry Awards website, 2006.

A version of "Twenty Lost Years" was presented at the Bronwen Wallace Conference in Kingston in 2009.

"Bess & Lloyd," "Praxia," & "Verulam" (all in earlier versions) appeared in the chapbook *Verulam* from above/ground press, 2009.

"Easter, 1916" (William Butler Yeats); "For The Union Dead" (Robert Lowell); "They Feed They Lion" (Philip Levine); "I Knew I'd Sing" (Heather McHugh)

"A Small Sacrifice," then titled "A Blunt Garde," was originally presented at the U of T course, "Influency," 2009; much revised it appears on the AngelHousePress website, 2010; under its new title, is has been revised further.

Thanks to: Margaret Christakos, Amanda Earl, Mark Goldstein, Sue Goyette, Bruce Hunter, rob mclennan, Carolyn Smart, Steven Ross Smith.

*

Avison, Margaret. *History of Ontario.* (Toronto: Gage, 1951).

Berg, Aase. *It's Not Acceptable to be Fatso.* www.actionbooks.org.

Berry, Wendell. *Standing by Words.* (San Francisco: North Point, 1983).

Broadfoot, Barry. *Ten Lost Years 1929–1939: Memories of Canadians Who Survived The Depression.* (New York: Doubleday, 1973).

Char, René. *Selected Poems.* Edited by Mary Ann Caws & Tina Jolas. (New York: New Directions, 1992).

Davenport, Guy. *Every Force Evolves A Form: Twenty Essays.* (San Francisco: North Point Press, 1987).

Grant, George. *Lament For a Nation.* (Toronto: M&S, 1965).

Hall, Tom T. *I Can't Dance / I Remember the Year Clayton Delaney Died* (song lyrics).

Innis, Harold Adams. *The Bias of Communication.* (Toronto: U of T Press, 1964).

———. *Empire and Communications.* 1950. Ed. David Godfrey. (Victoria, B.C.: Press Porcepic, 1986).

Jabès, Edmund. *The Little Book of Unsuspected Subversion.* Translated by Rosemarie Waldrop. (Stanford: Stanford University Press, 1996).

Lee, Dennis. *Civil Elegies.* (Toronto: Anansi, 1968).

Livesay, Dorothy. *The Documentaries.* (Toronto: Ryerson, 1968).

Middleton, Peter. *Distant Reading: Performance, Readership, and Consumption in Contemporary Poetry.* (Tuscaloosa: The University of Alabama Press, 2005).

Miłosz, Czesław. *The Captive Mind.* Translated by Jane Zielonko. (London: Secker & Warburg, 1953).

Morson, Gary Saul, Caryl Emerson. *Mikhail Bakhtin: Creation of a Prosaics.* (Stanford: University Press, 1990).

Paz, Octavio. *Alternating Current.* (New York: Viking, 1973).

———. *The Other Voice: Essays on Modern Poetry.* (New York: Harcourt Brace, 1990).

Trilling, Lionel. *Sincerity and Authenticity.* (Cambridge: Harvard University Press: 1972).

Wallace, Bronwen. *The Stubborn Particulars of Grace.* (Toronto: M&S, 1987).

Zukofsky, Louis. *Prepositions: The Collected Critical Essays.* (New York: Horizon Press, 1968).

∼

A NOTE ON THE TYPE

Typeset in ITC New Baskerville and John Sans. New Baskerville is a font family based on a type design created in 1724 by John Baskerville of Birmingham, England. A historically important font, Baskerville helped bridge the transition from Old Style to Modern typefaces. John Sans is a new grotesk developed at the Storm Type Foundry in Czech by type designer František Štorm. John Sans is monolinear in character with fine shadings and softenings that benefit both its legibility and aesthetics.

Type+Design: www.beautifuloutlaw.com

COLOPHON

Manufactured fall 2011 by BookThug in an edition of 500 copies.
Distributed in Canada by the Literary Press Group: www.lpg.ca
Distributed in the USA by Small Press Distribution: www.spdbooks.org
Shop on-line at www.bookthug.ca

BOOK
PRODUCTION
WAR ECONOMY
STANDARD

11 12 13 14 · 5 4 3 2